Kevin at the Vet

by Holly Harper
illustrated by Leo Trinidad

OXFORD
UNIVERSITY PRESS

Kevin and Tala go on a jog.

Kevin is not well.

Off to visit the vet.

Jen will fix him.

Jess the duck is at the vet.

Kevin is in his box.

Kevin and Jess can relax.

She is wet in the tub.

Wag! Wag! He is well.

I can pick up Kevin.

Kevin will not go.
Jess is his pal.

I will fix Kevin and Jess.

Jess is in the van.

Tala, Jess and Kevin go on a jog.

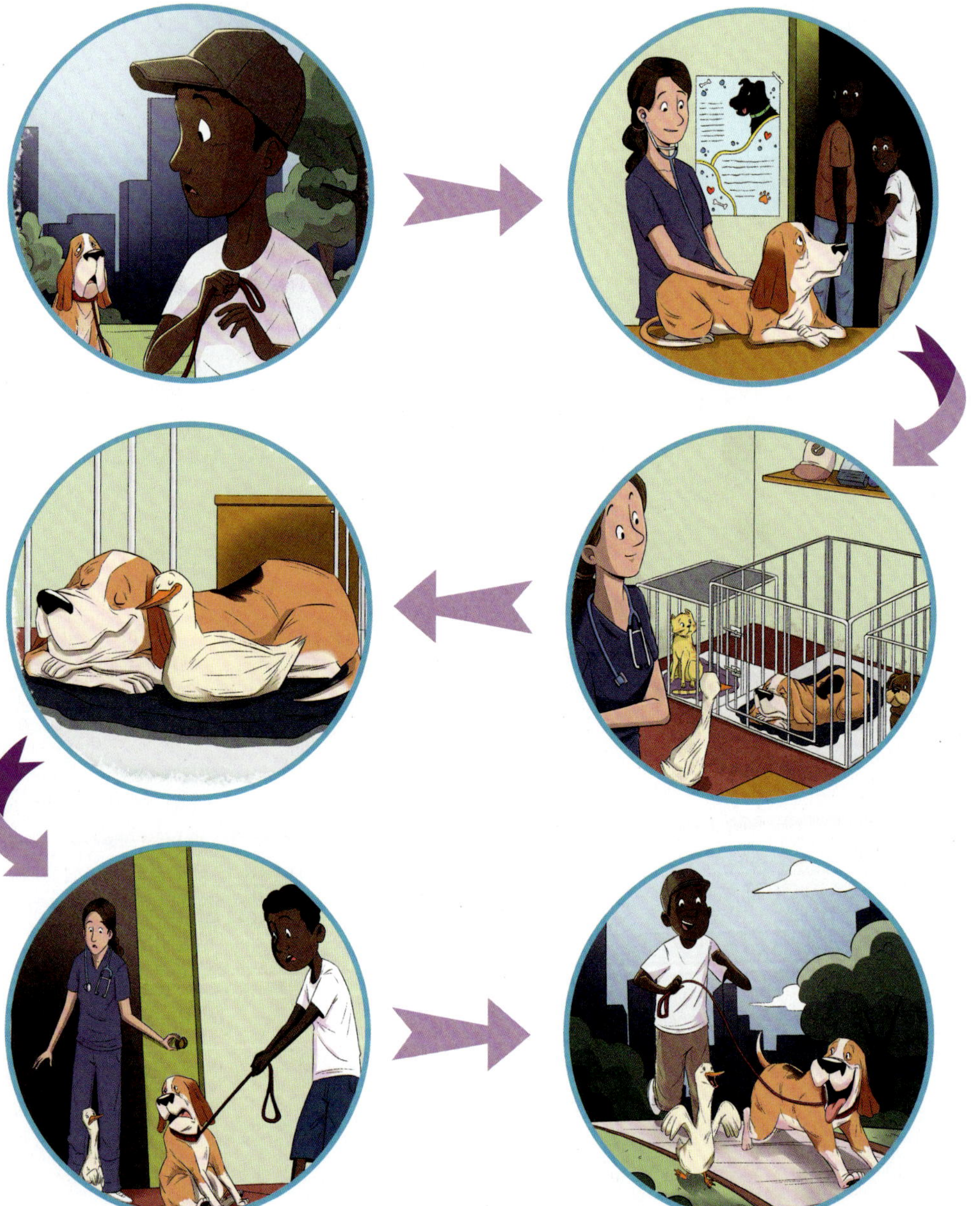

Encourage students to use the pictures to retell the story.